HEAVY PETTING

Romantic Advice from my Cat

Bumper

HEAVY PETTING

Romantic Advice from my Cat

Bumper

Liz Nickles and Tamara Asseyer
Illustrated by Bonnie Timmons

HYPERION
NEW YORK

Library of Congress Cataloging-in-Publication Data

Nickles, Elizabeth.
    Heavy petting : romantic advice from my cat / Liz Nickles and Tamara
Asseyev : illustrated by Bonnie Timmons.
        p.   cm.
    ISBN 1-56282-799-5
    1. Cats—Humor. 2. Sex—Humor. 3. American wit and humor.
Pictorial. I. Asseyev, Tamara. II. Timmons, Bonnie. III. Title.
PN6231.C23N55   1994
741.5'973—dc20
                                              93-26407
                                              CIP

FIRST EDITION

10 9 8 7 6 5 4 3 2 1

Meet your mate

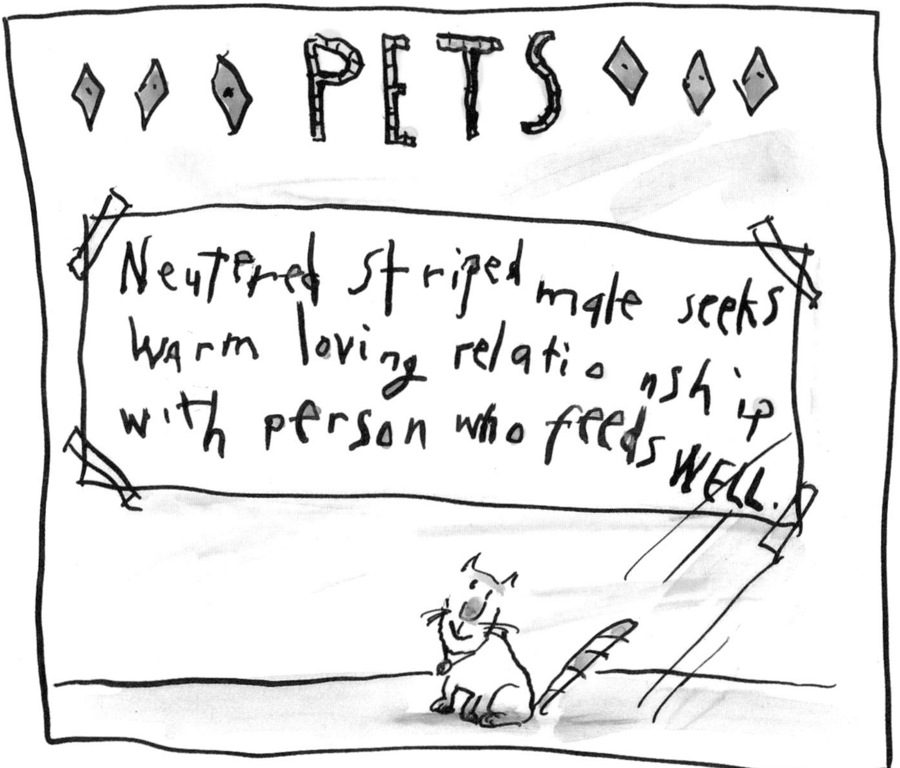
PETS
Neutered striped male seeks
warm loving relationship
with person who feeds WELL.

Try singles ads

Hang out where the prospects are

Have a romantic encounter

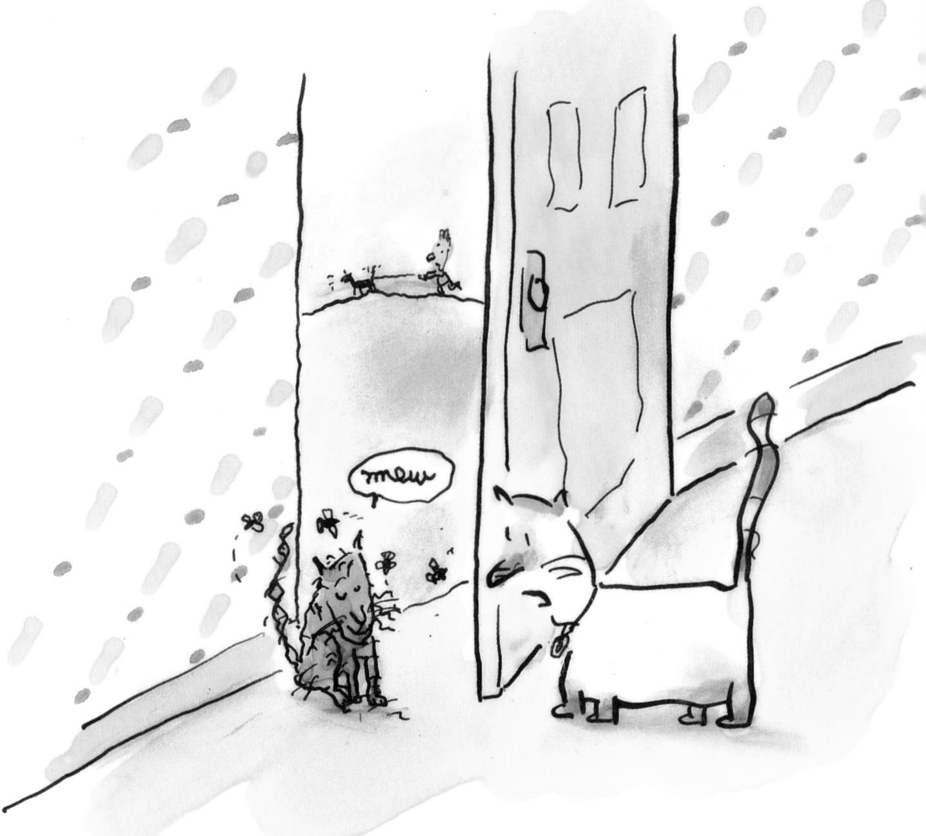
mew

Have a blind date

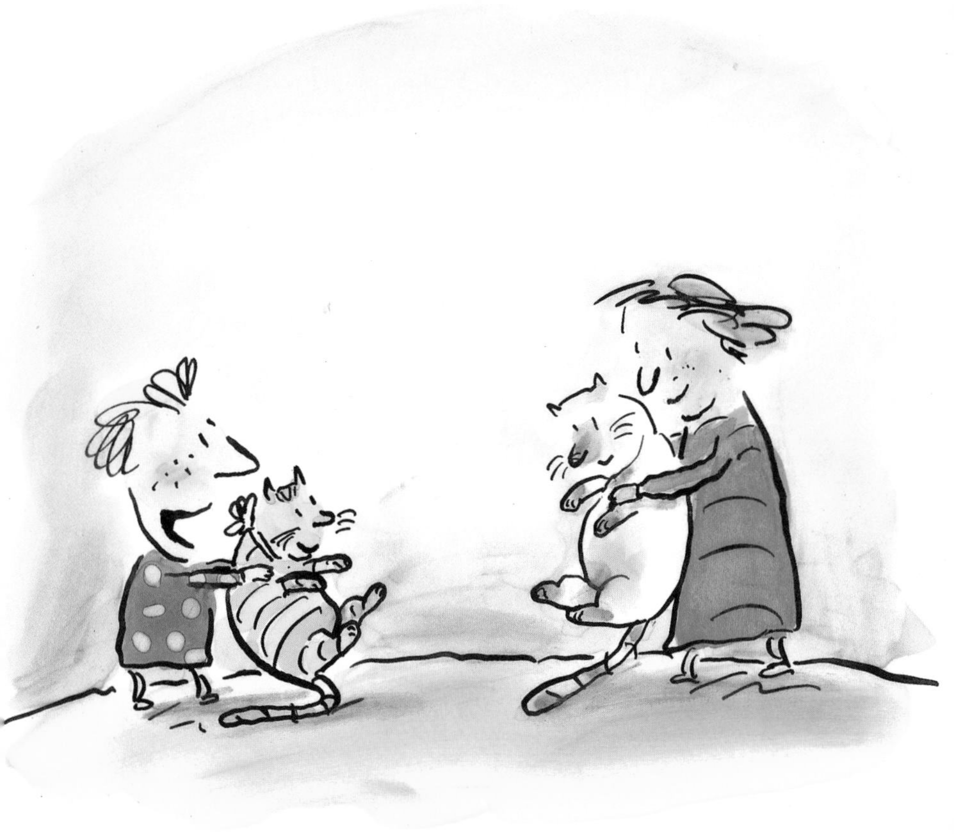

Let friends fix you up

Dating do's and don'ts

DO: Sniff each other out

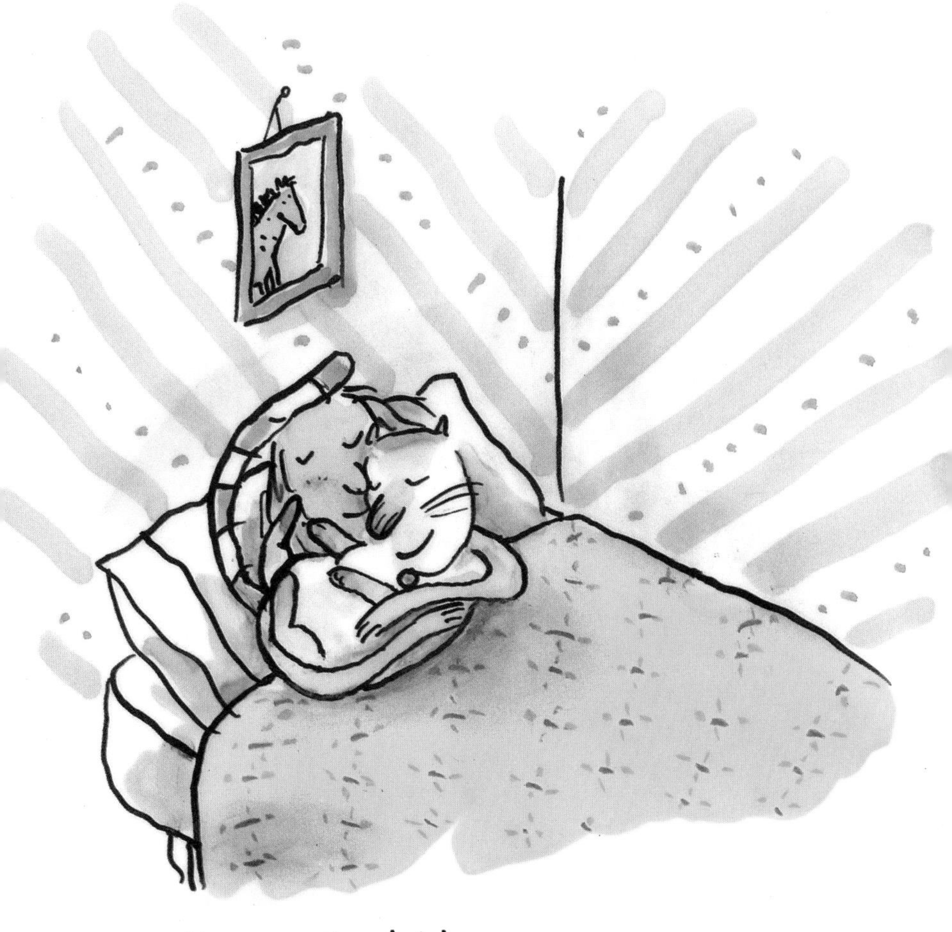

Do: Cuddle

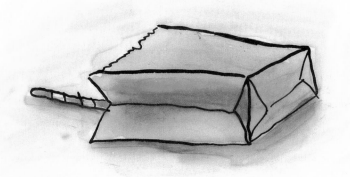

DO: Maintain mystery

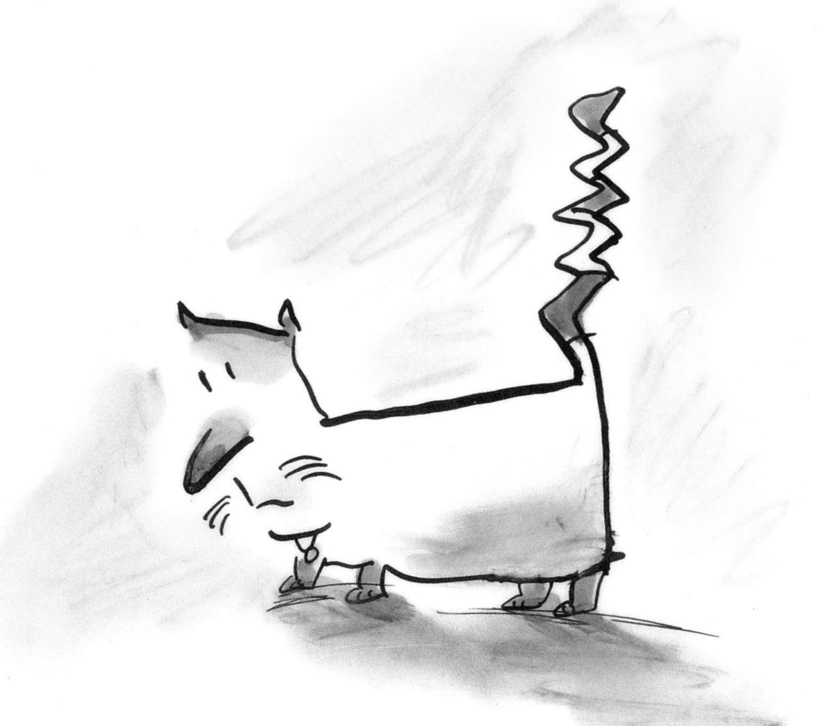

DO: Get kinky

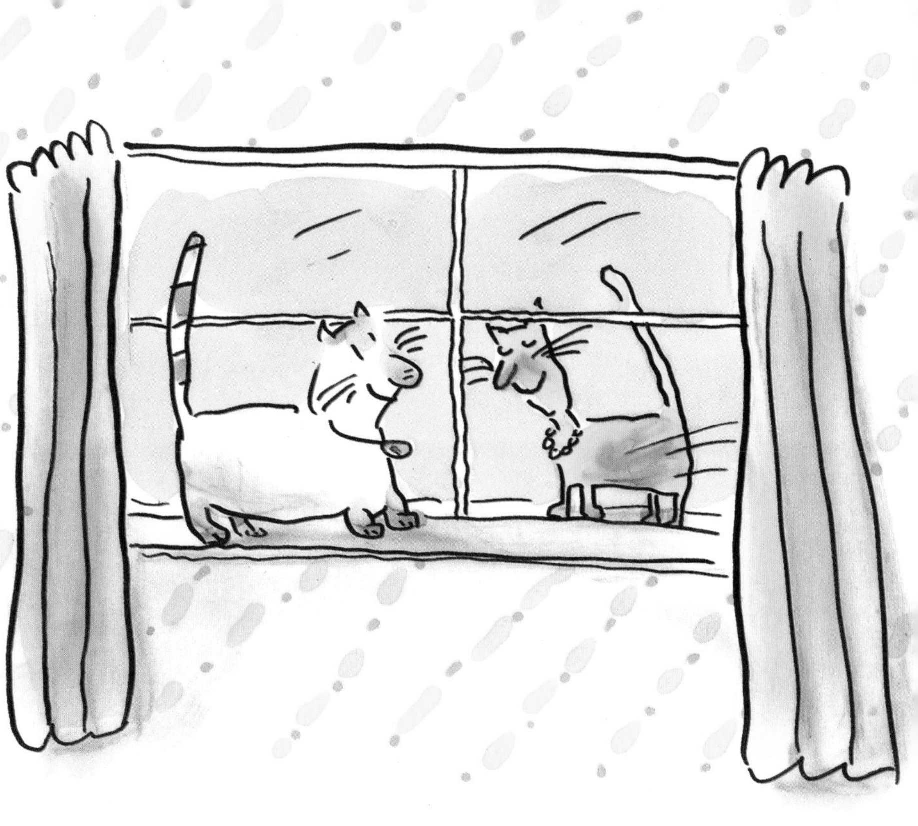

DO: Practice safe sex

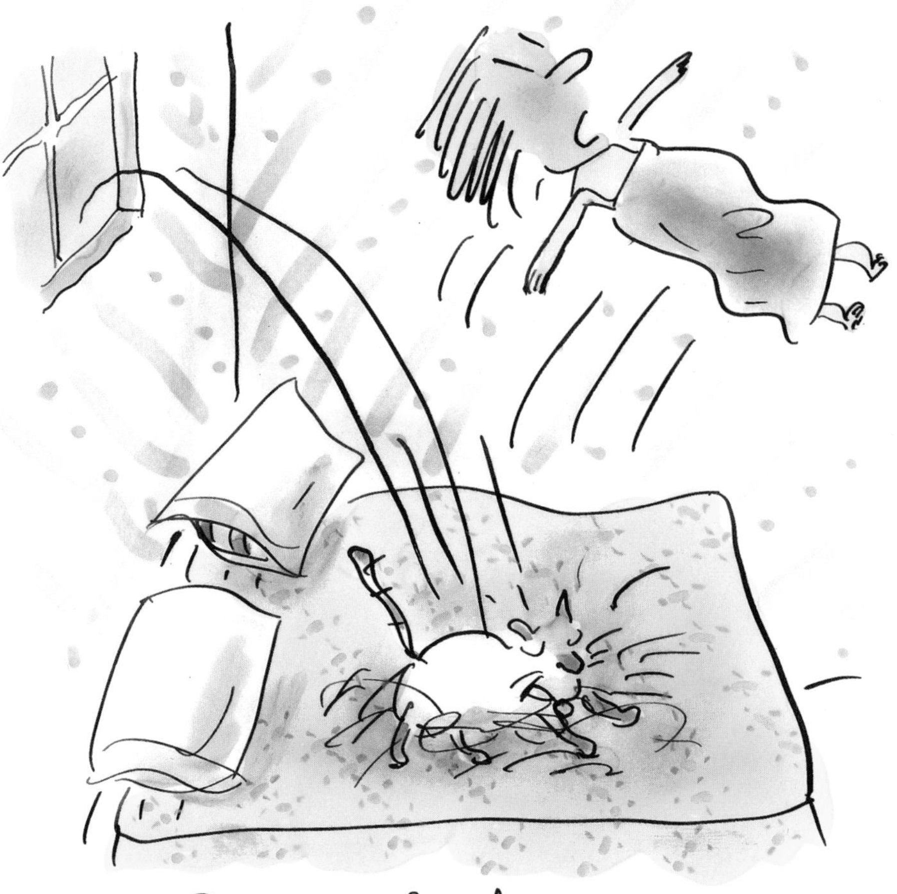

DON'T: Bedhop

DON'T: Get a headache

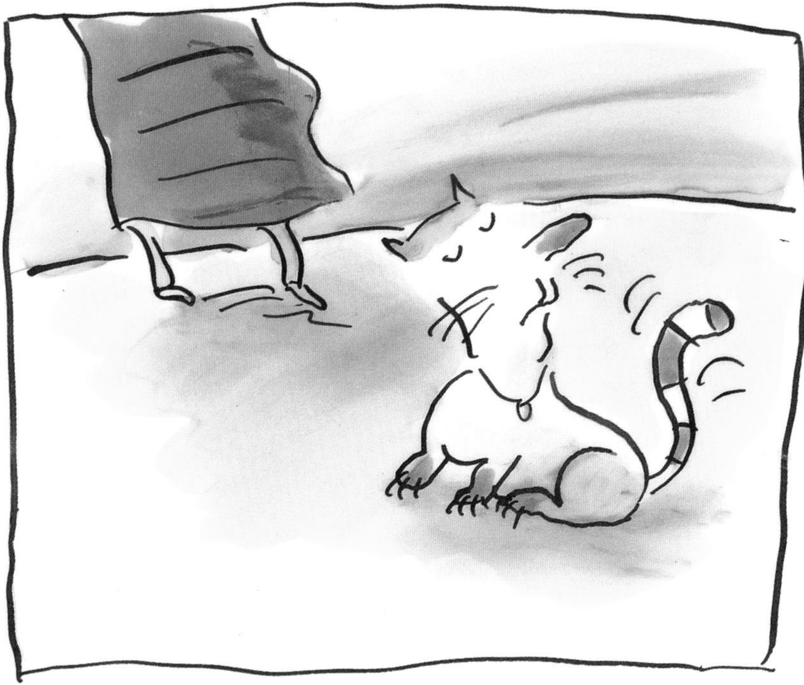

DON'T: Be catty

DON'T: Clam up

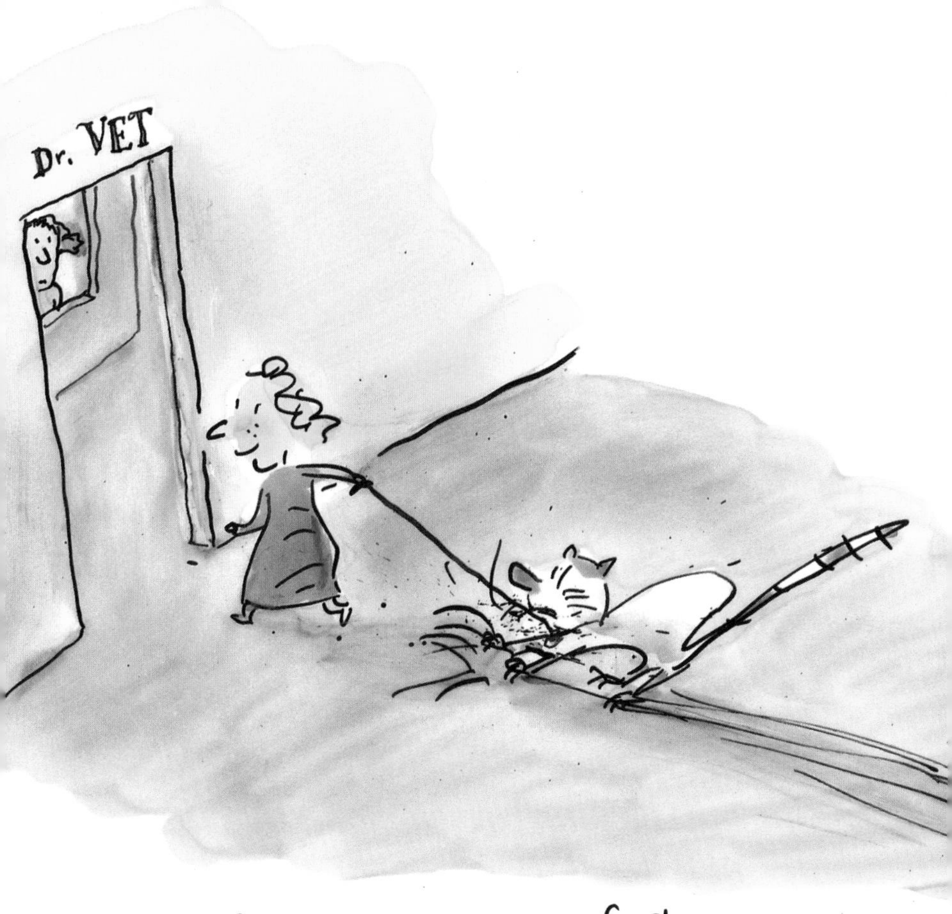
Dr. VET

DONT: Drag your feet

Winning wiles and ways

Give good massage

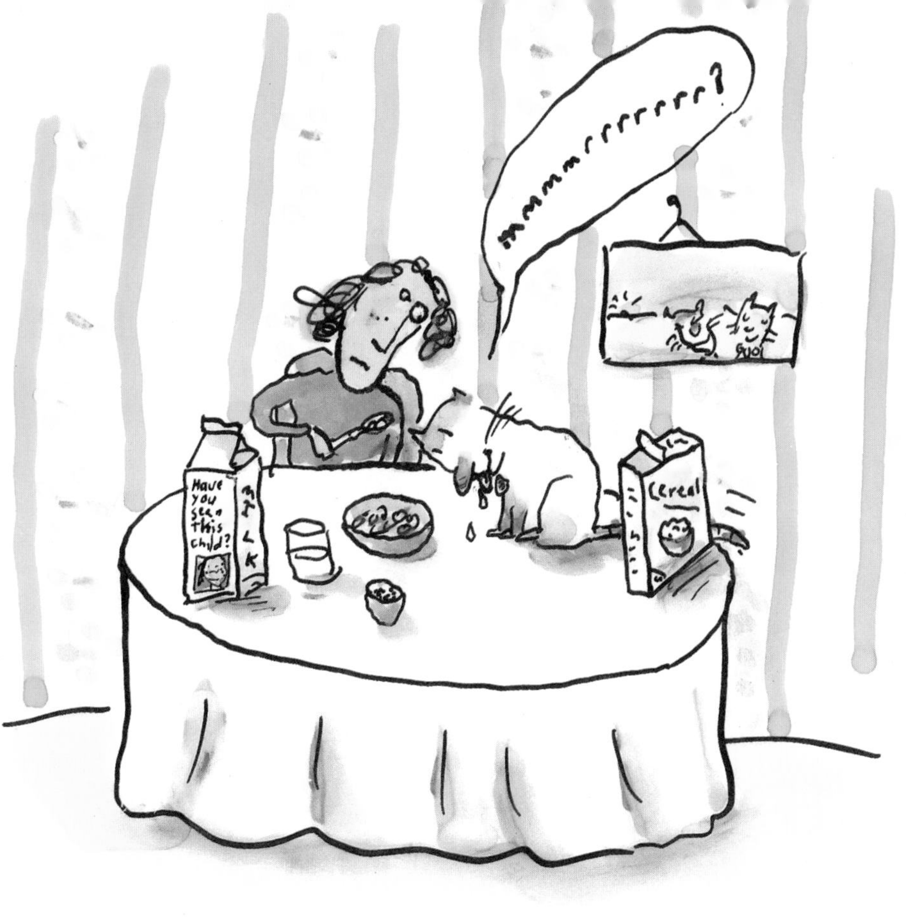
mmmmrrrrrrr?
Have you seen this child?
MILK
Cereal

Talk at breakfast

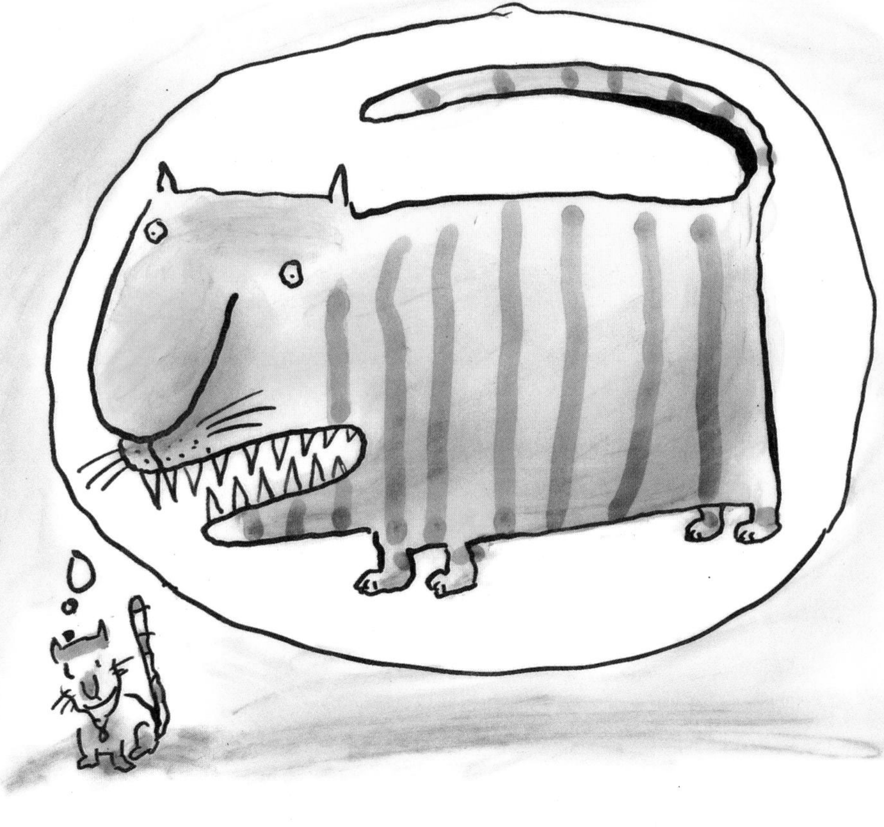

Think big

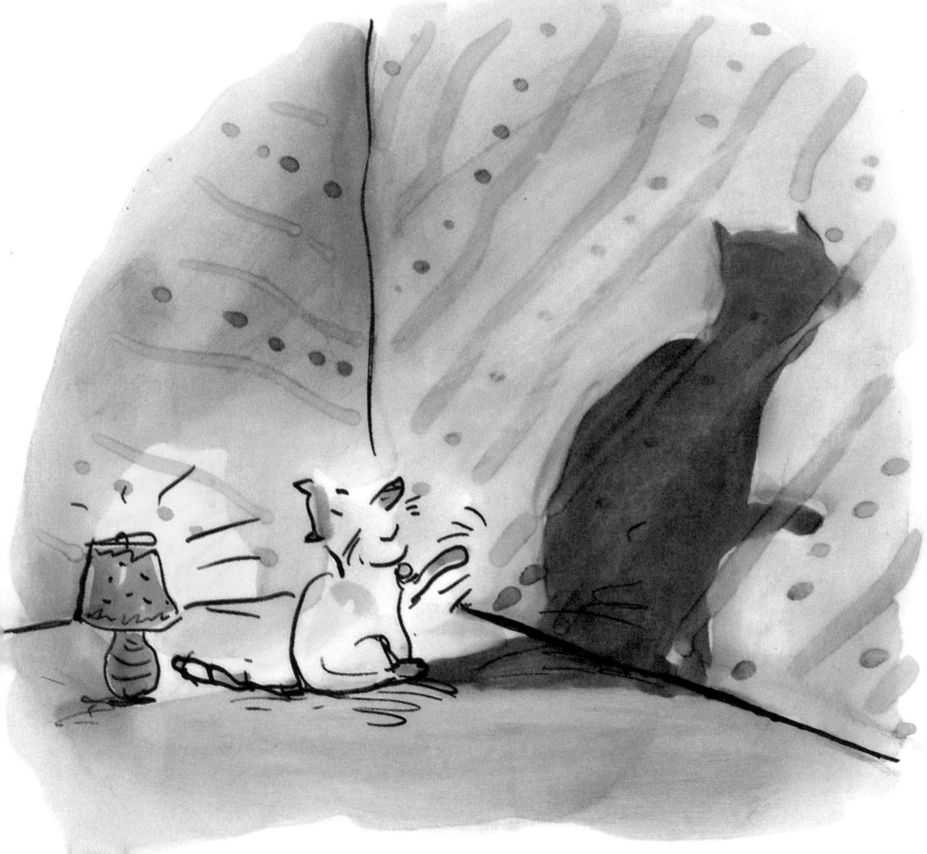

Be entertaining

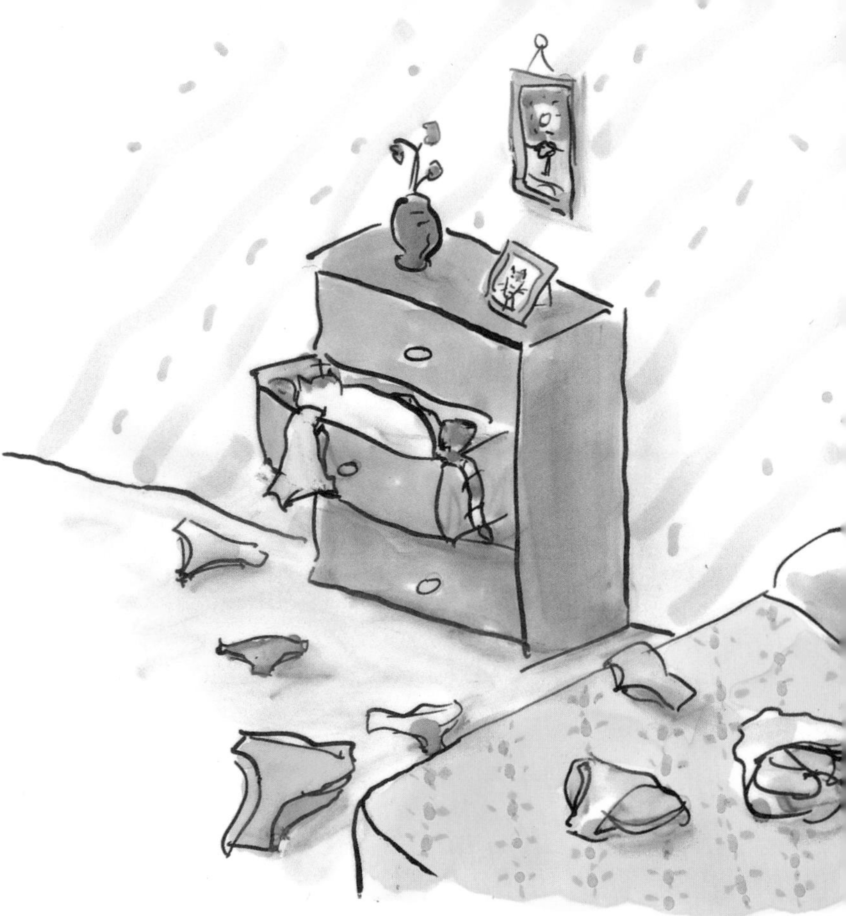

Wear clean undies

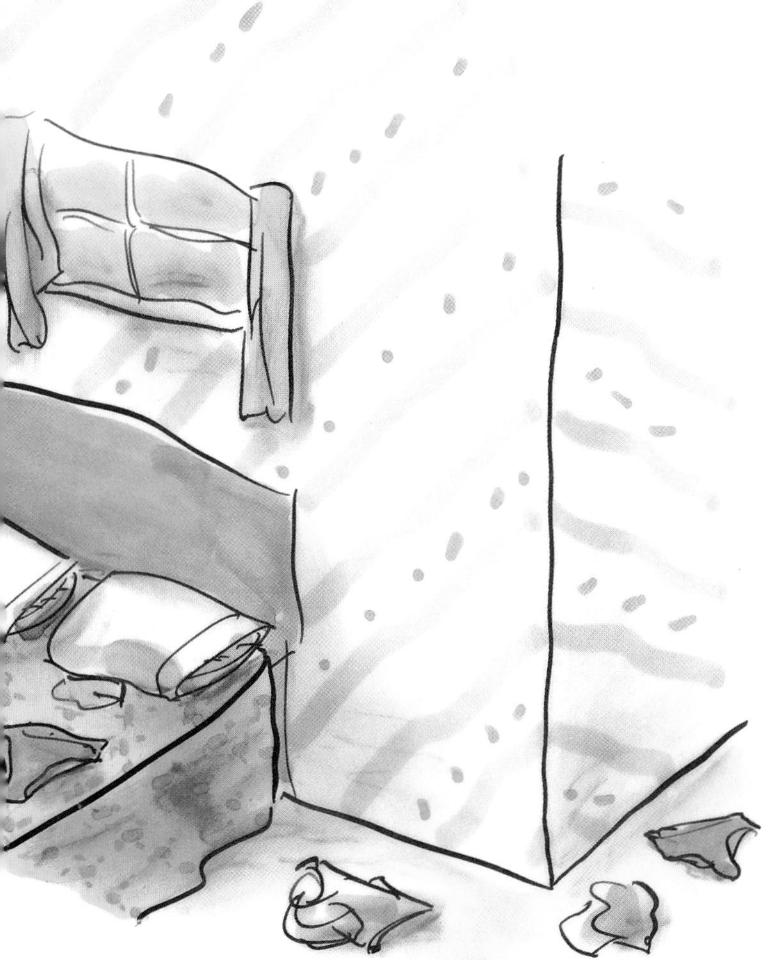

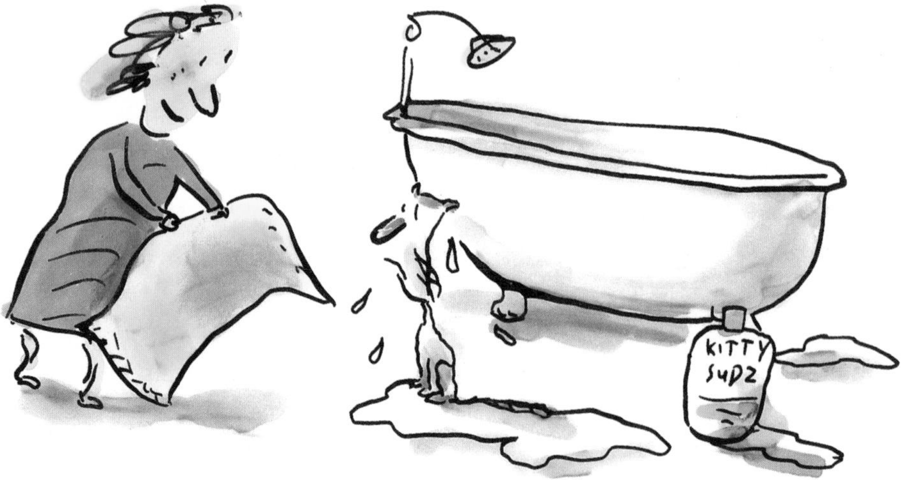
KITTY
SUDZ

Get made over

Play the dating game

Be a trophy date

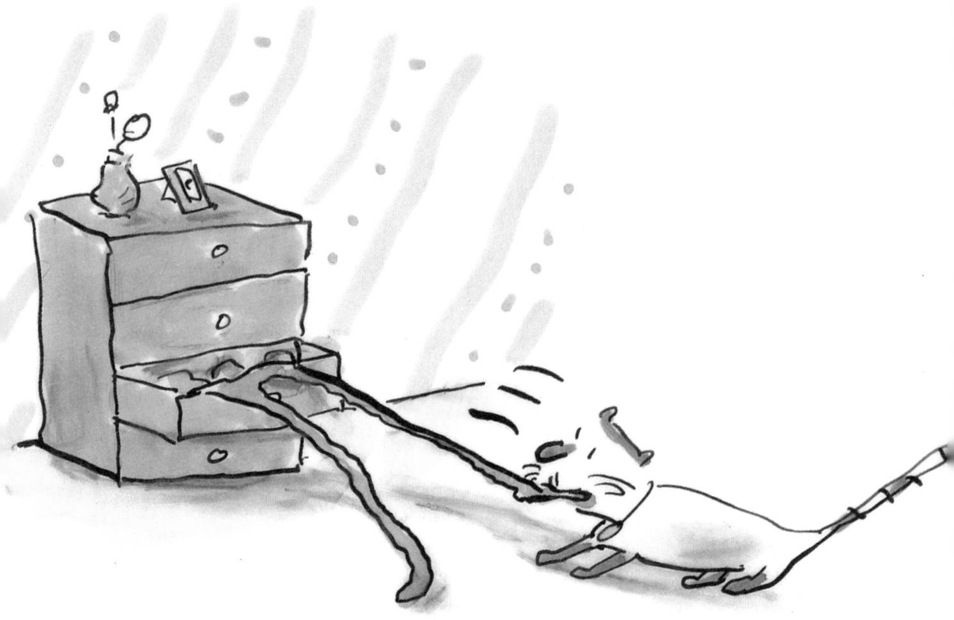

Wear pantyhose.

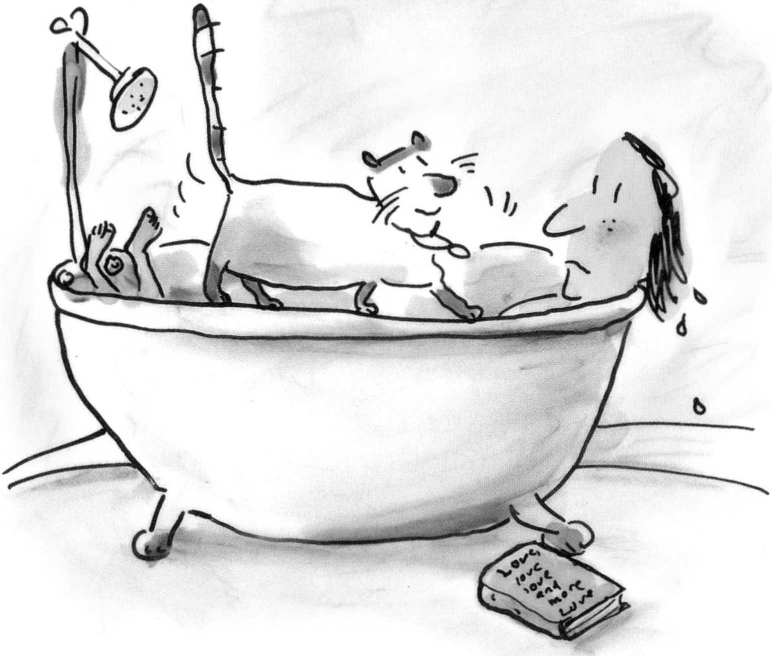
Love, love love and more Love

Show off

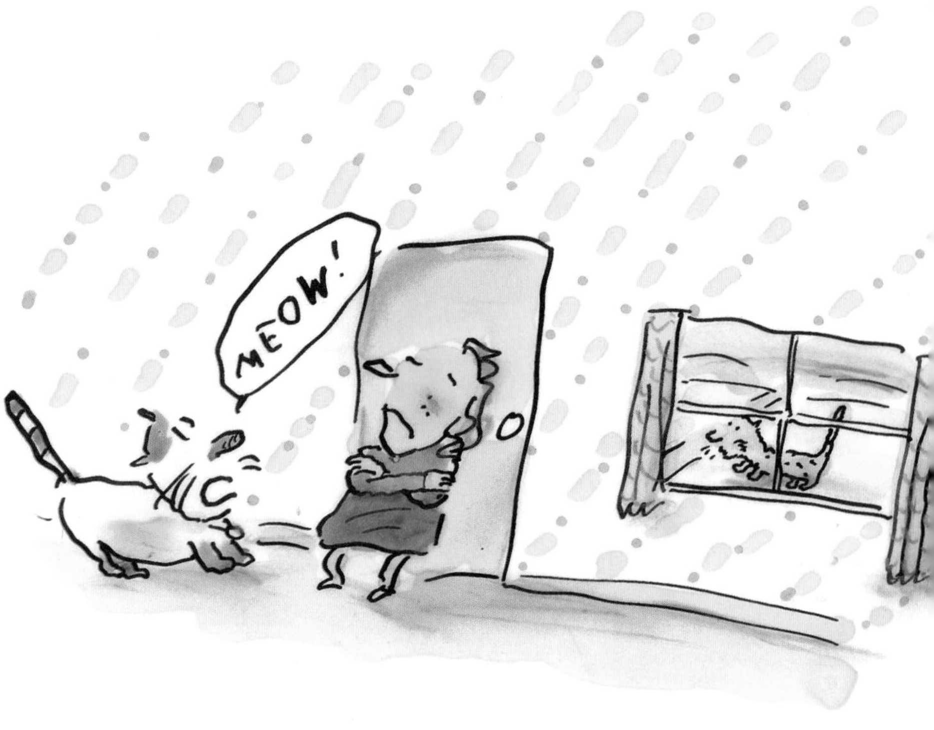
MEOW!

Celibacy

Monotony

Monogamy

Bigamy

Polygamy

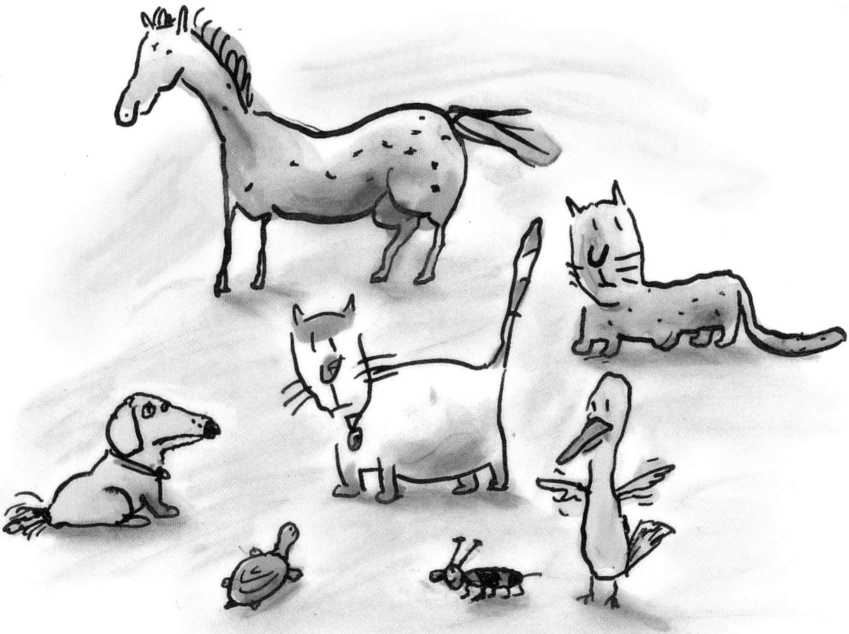

Menagerie

Foreplay is the cat's meow

Kiss till you're tongue-tied

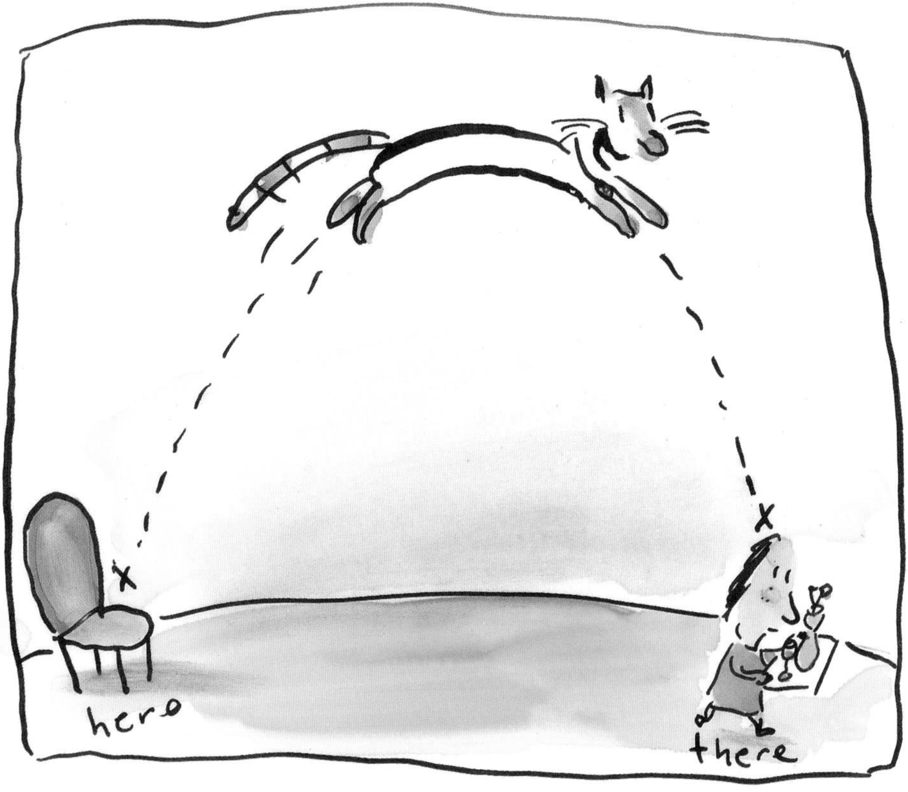
here
there

Practice your pounce

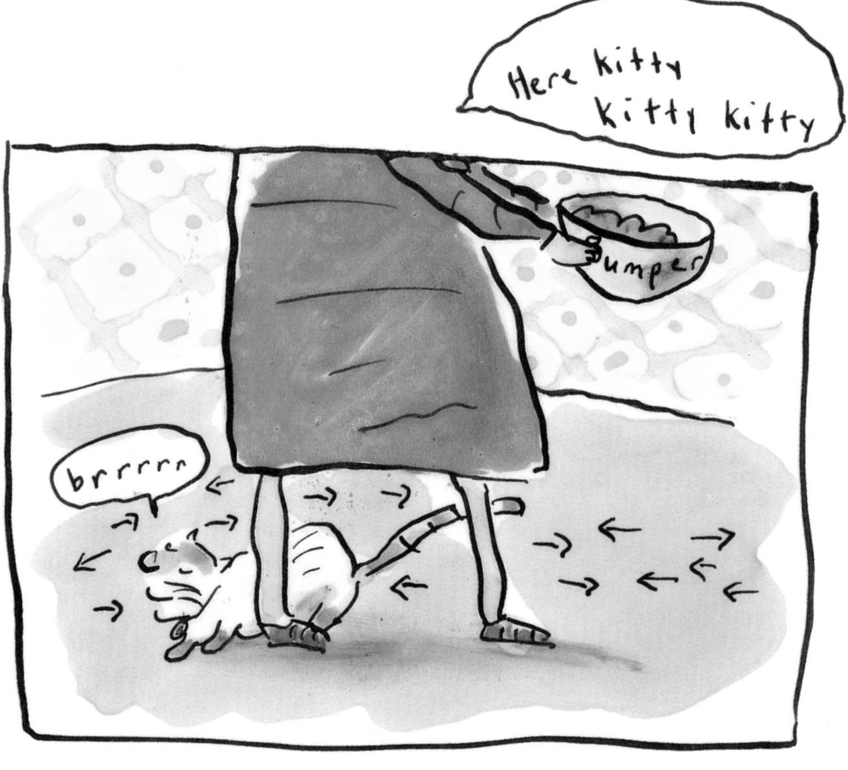
Here kitty kitty kitty
brrrrrr
umper

Legs are for rubbing

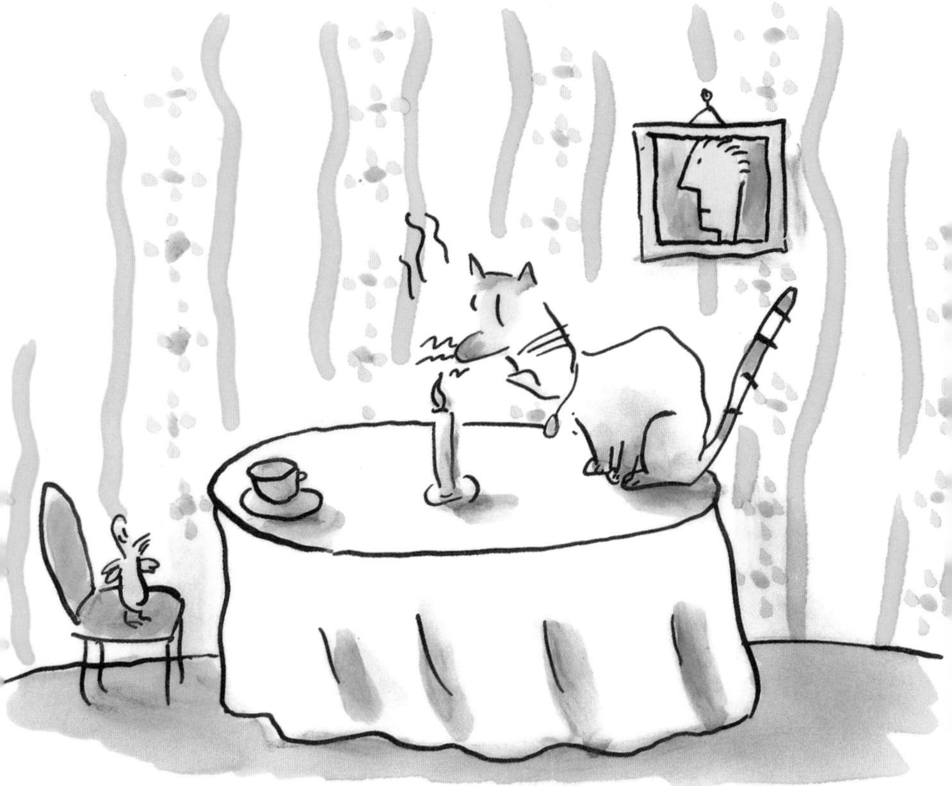

Avoid whisker burn

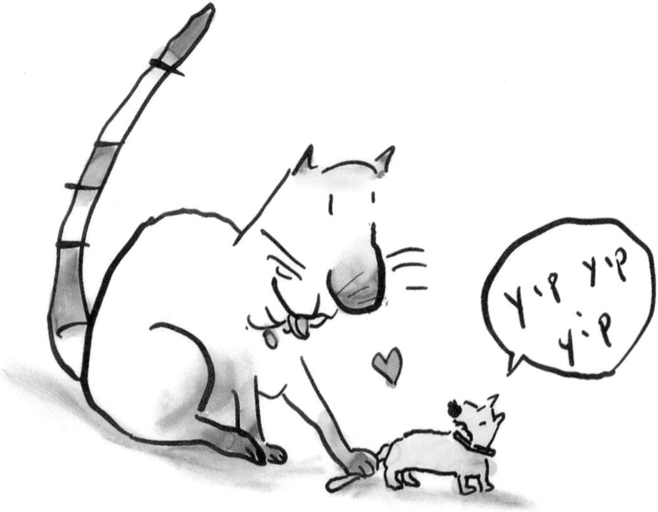
yip yip
yip

Opposites attract

Know your erogenous zones

Practice the art of petting

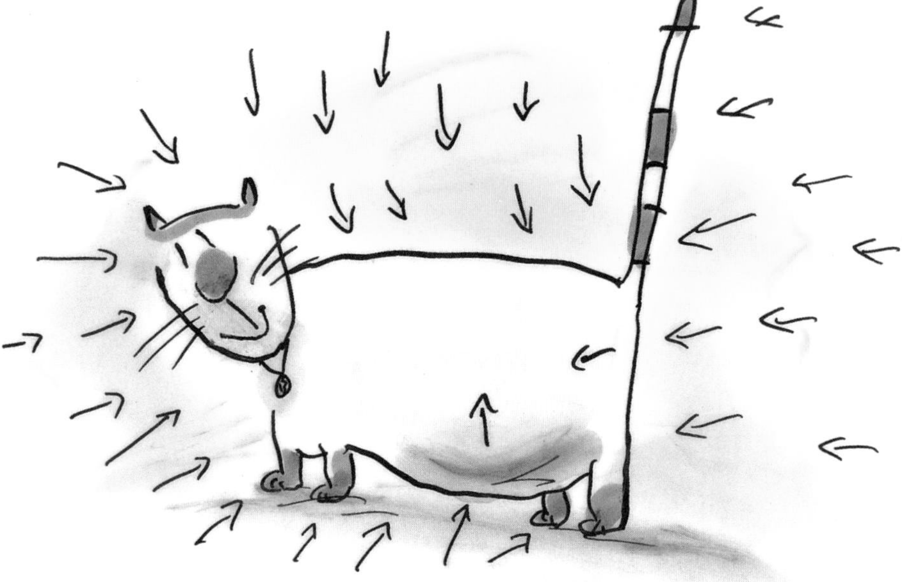

Where to pet

guide to aphrodisiacs

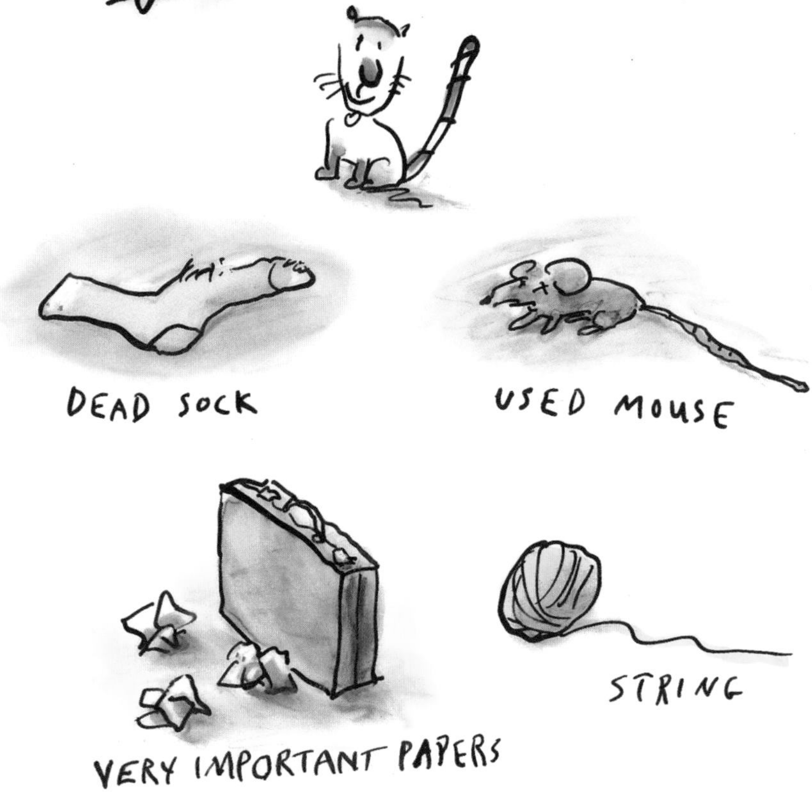
DEAD SOCK
USED MOUSE
VERY IMPORTANT PAPERS
STRING

Sex toys

ANYTHING
AROUND

EXPENSIVE
JEWELRY

CURTAINS

BUGS

... more sex toys

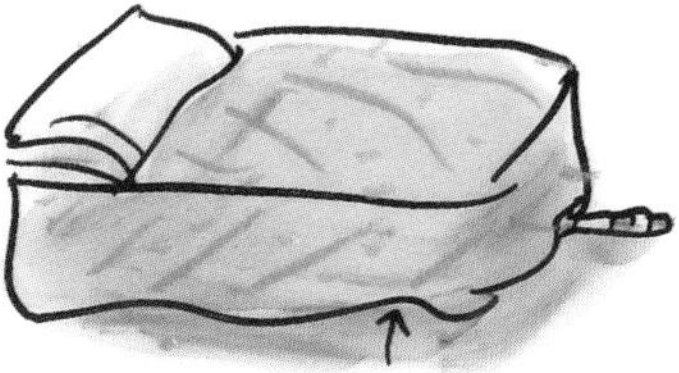

UNDER BED

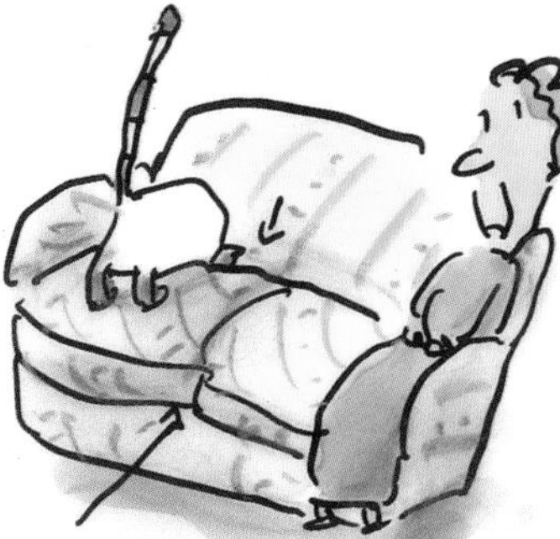

BETWEEN CUSHIONS

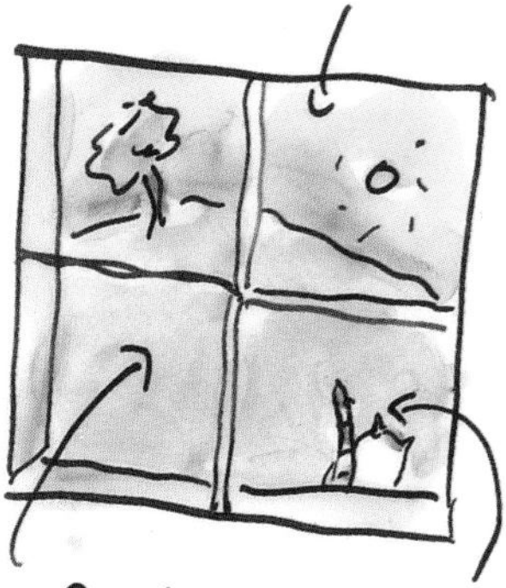

BACK YARD

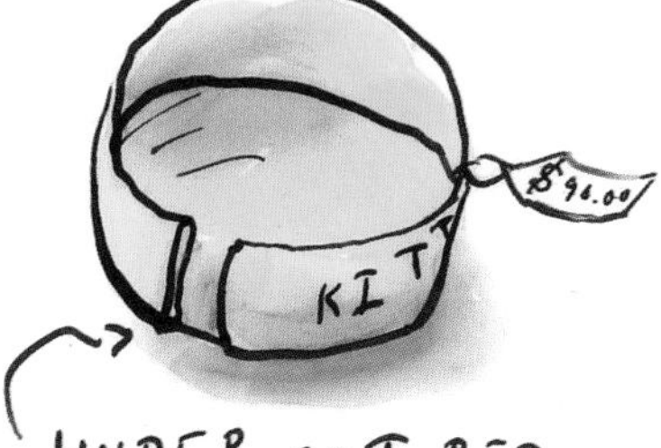

$96.00
KITT

UNDER CAT BED
(never used)

And places to hide them

Beware perversions

Phone sex

Exhibitionism

Ménage à trois

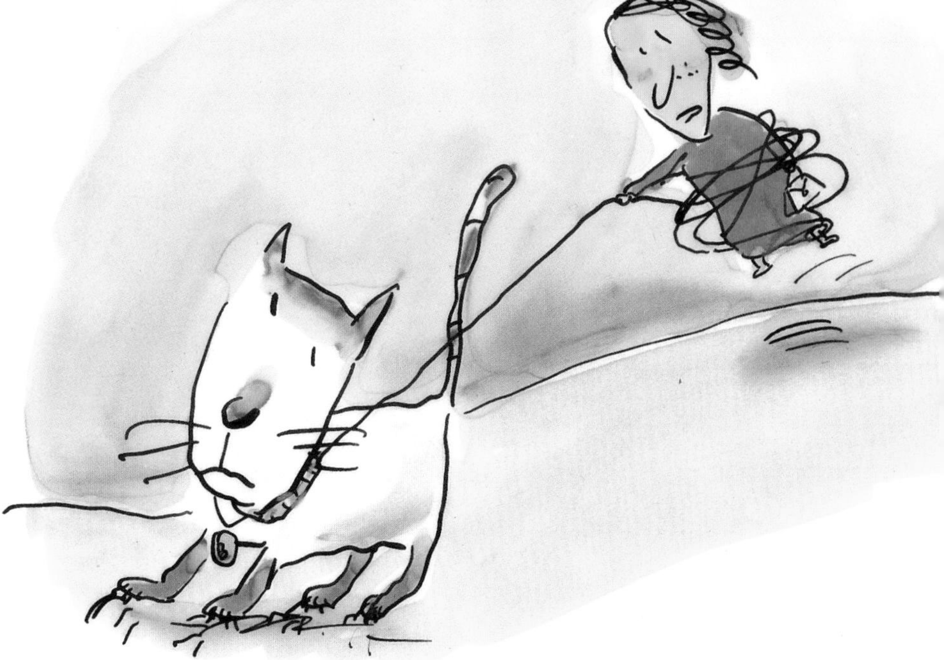

Bondage

Beware fatal attractions

Turn-ons are for trying

Position 1

Position 2

Position 5

Position 4

Practice erotic positions

Rough licking

Hairy chests

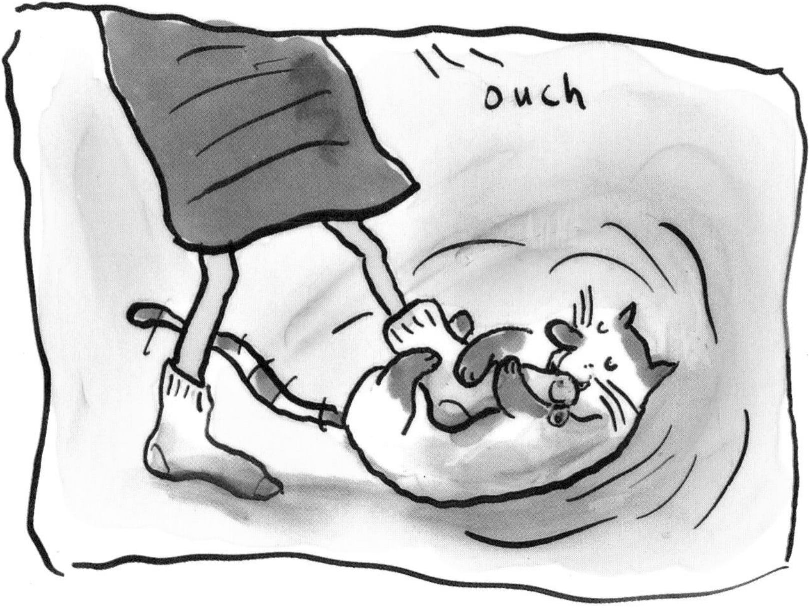
ouch

Love bites

Playing with yourself can be fun

TUNA

SALTINES

ICE CREAM

VELVET

FUR

Aphrodisiacs

Feline fantasies

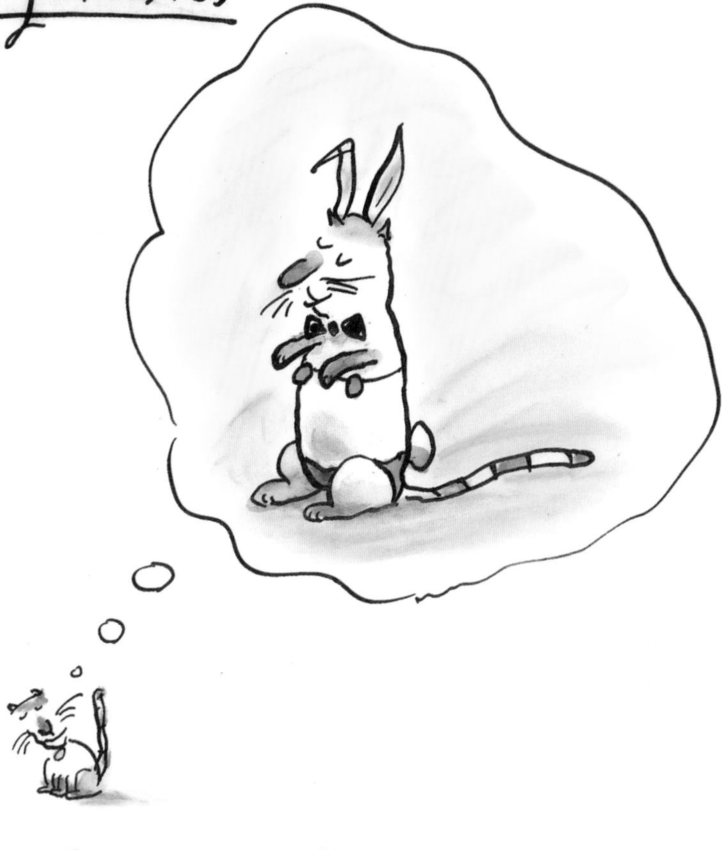

Be a sex object

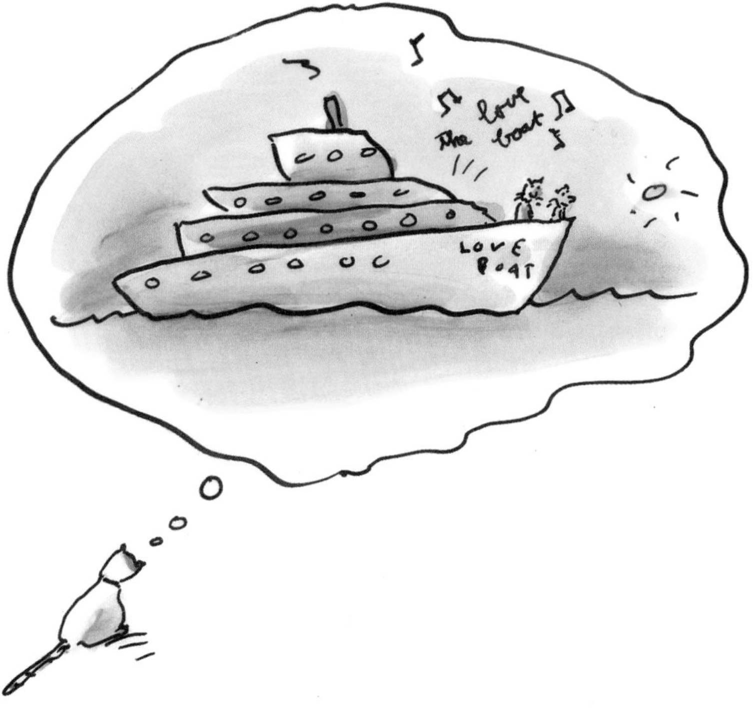
love the boat
LOVE BOAT

Cruise on the Love Boat

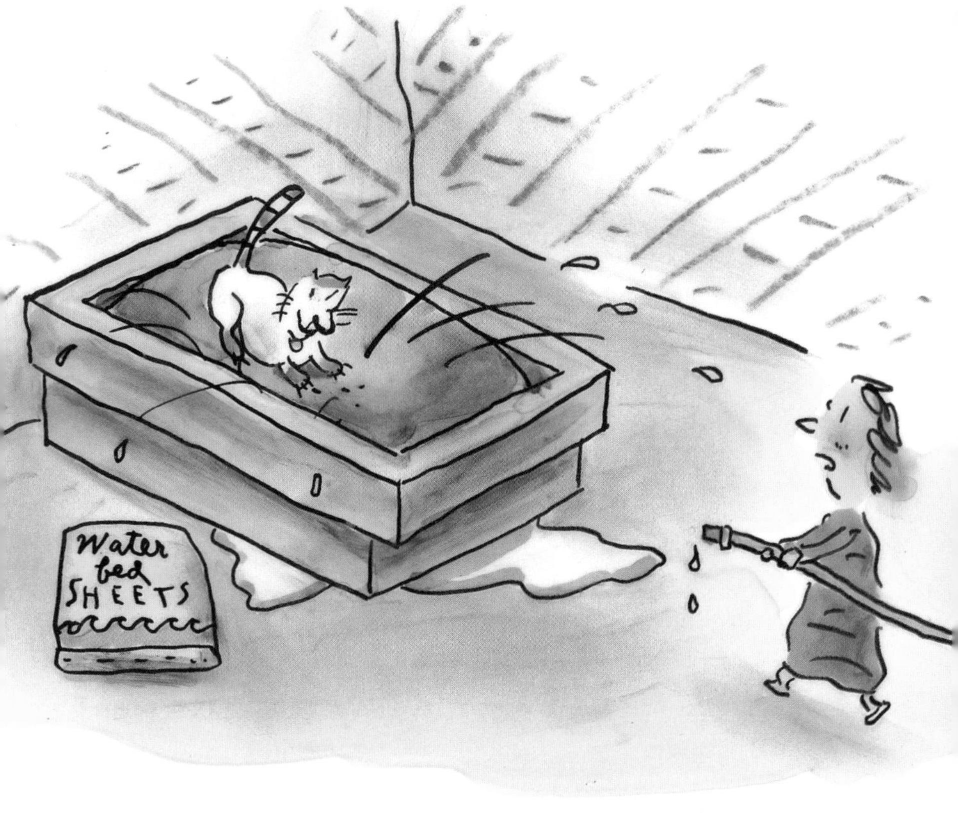
Water
bed
SHEETS

Get a bigger, better bed

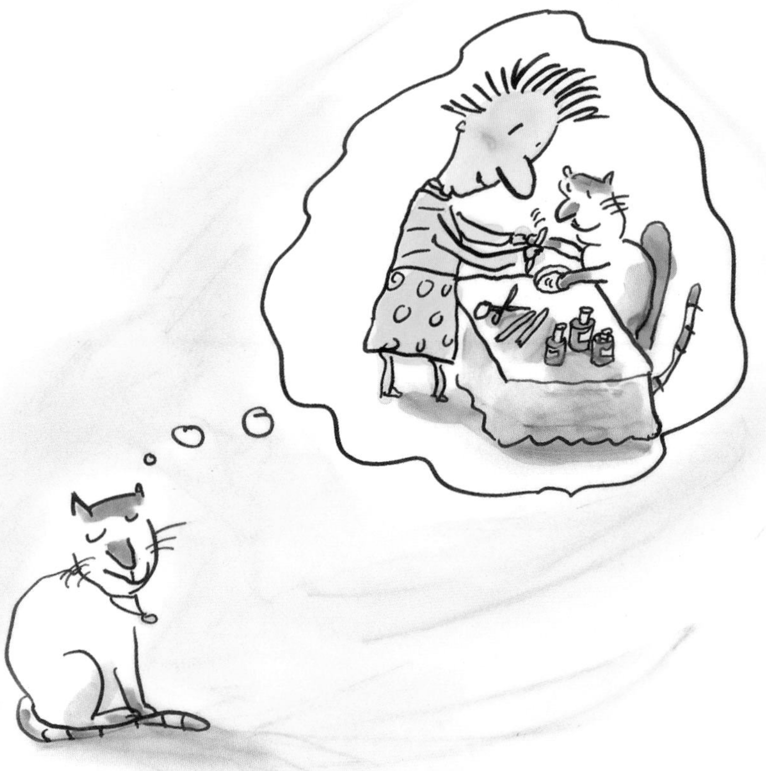

Get a fantasy makeover

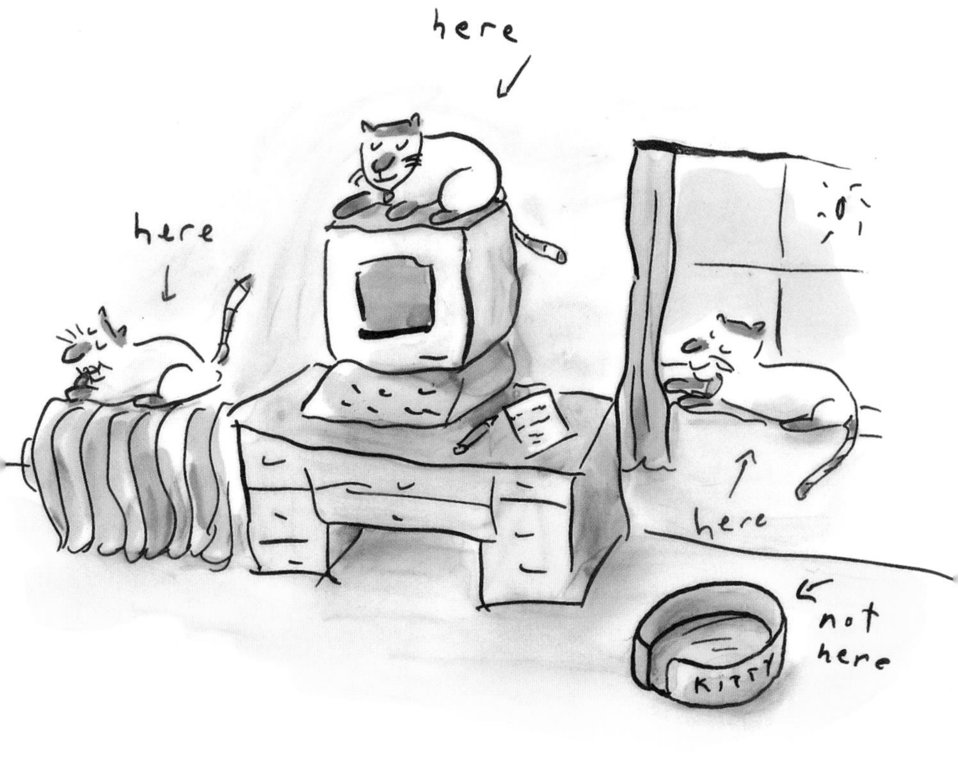
here
here
here
not here
KITTY

Home office sexy spots

Breaking up

1. Eat
2. Sleep
3. Eat
4. Sleep
5. Eat
6. Sleep

Emotional addiction and recovery:
A 12-step program

7. Eat

8. Sleep

9. Eat

10. sleep

11. Eat

12. sleep

Don't cry over spilt milk